Island Experiences

Adventures in Bocas del Toro, on the Caribbean coast of Panama

by

Maible Matrishon

Island Experiences

Maible Matrishon

Copyright © 2013 by Maible Matrishon

Cover art copyright © 2013 by Maible Matrishon

Published by Matrishon Media

MaibleMatrishon.com

Contents

Prologue	1
Chapter 1 - The Beginning	3
Chapter 2 - Time to Start Building	7
Chapter 3 - Meeting Friends	8
Chapter 4 - Who Do I Ask?	9
Chapter 5 - A Nice Day at the Island	10
Chapter 6 - Exploring the Area	12
Chapter 7 - One Year Later	15
Chapter 8 - Bocas Net and Other Things	17
Chapter 9 - A Busy Social Calendar	19
Chapter 10 -Tiles	21
Chapter 11 - A Breakfast with Johne and Aeon	24
Chapter 12 - A Nice Horse Adventure	28
Chapter 13 - Kathy's Party	31
Epilogue	33
About The Author	35

Additional material and photographs illustrating "Island Experiences" available at:-

MaibleMatrishon.com

Prologue

My name is Maible Matrishon. I have always liked writing, but I never thought I was going to get the privilege to write a book myself.

I was inspired to write this book by a famous mystery writer by the name of Agatha Christie. I had heard of Agatha, then one day my mom told me that she was related to me by marriage. Here is a bit of history on Agatha Christie.

Agatha Christie never attended school, she was only taught by the occasional tutor. She first decided to occupy herself with music and started writing later on in life.

Agatha Christie wrote her first detective novel while working for a hospital during World War 1. The novel (Murder in Mesopotamia) was completed in a year, but it only got published five years later.

Agatha Christie wrote more than sixty-six novels. She wrote short stories, screen plays and a series of romantic novels. When she wrote the romantic novels she went by the name of Mary Westmacott. Her books have been translated into more than a hundred different languages.

Agatha Christie was the most popular mystery writer of all times.

Although my story is fictitious, it is based on real life events. I started writing this story just for fun, but then I decided I wanted to make it into a real book. As part of home schooling at the island, I had a Heritage Fair project on which to work. I wanted to publish this book, following in the footsteps of Agatha Christie.

Chapter 1

The Beginning

I was at my favourite restaurant, Tropical Bird. It was in Bocas Del Toro, Panama. I was eating my favourite dish, a decent sized plate of rice and beans with veggies. The restaurant was quite quiet for a Friday afternoon; it was usually bustling with people by now.

I had been to Panama before, and to Tropical Bird. I was down here again, to buy an island.

The only people still at Tropical Bird were a couple. I thought they were from England, judging by their heavy accents. I told the waitress that I wanted a coffee with milk (cafe con leche), she waved me away saying she would get it soon.

I went to get a Bocas Breeze, the local paper, from the corner where they keep multiple types of magazines. I got the latest paper so I could catch-up on the daily news. There was not much on the news that was interesting, just all the usual things like advertisements for surf schools, restaurants that were already out of business and so on.

When I had finished my meal and read the whole Bocas Breeze, both Spanish and English, I went back to the hotel in which I was staying.

It was a nice hotel with clean rooms and a nice deck overlooking the water. It also had a great view of Isla Caranero, a beautiful island with a couple nice restaurants on the water and a marina.

I finally fell asleep, but an hour later I was woken up by a small, but lively rumble and the sound of waves very, very close to the floor. I could just picture water coming up through all the little cracks. There was a big storm! The thunder was so loud and the lighting looked like it was very close. I wanted to go back to sleep and forget about it but it kept me awake for the rest of the night! The storm stopped by 6:00am.

I knew it was early, but I got up and searched town for a coffee shop that was open. I found one on a little side street. Their coffee tasted more like cleaning fluid than coffee to me, but I still drank it.

After I had finished my coffee I went to the main street and bought some apples from a street vendor. I ate like a pig, not wasting a bit of the apple. I looked like a lost puppy, wandering around town thinking what to do next.

A man stopped me and started blathering on in fast Spanish. I just waved him away, not knowing what he was talking about. I was sure it was not important to me at the time.

I slowly found my way to a tour booth. I wanted to go to a fun beach a little ways out of town, if that was possible. I found a tour for 2:00pm. The bus would arrive at the beach (Starfish Beach) at 2:30. I could spend 4 hours wandering around the jungle and lying on sandy beaches. That sounded great to me.

I booked one ticket for thirty dollars, including snacks and drinks at a snack bar on the beach.

It was currently 1:00. I still did not know what to do for the next hour. I decided I would go back to my hotel and catch up on my sleep. I set my alarm for 1:30. I woke up to my alarm going ZING! ZING! ZING!

I put my clothes on and walked up to the tour station, only four blocks from my hotel. I got there just in time. I had my backpack filled with stuff like sunscreen, bug dope, bathing suit, towel. I was well set for the day, I thought.

The beach was quite nice. There were lots of starfish and fish and other cool creatures.

"I think I might stay on the beach for a while." I said to the tour guide, who was taking a group into the mangroves (so called The Jungle.) I went to the food and drink stand and got a ginger ale. I hung out on the beach for a while and went snorkelling for a bit.

"I will go in the jungle." I said to myself. I got my flip flops on and started climbing on long the leafy roots. I caught up to the guide. They were looking at the flower called "Up Side-Down Hibiscus".

It was a red flower with multiple petals. It looked like it was hanging upside down.

Then we kept walking, and the guide showed us termite mounds. I did not have to look, because like I said, I had been in Panama and I have gone through this process! I went off the trail a bit to see things I did not know about, including spider, birds, beetles and lizards. I asked the guide some questions about spiders, most importantly, which ones were poisonous and which were not.

"Excuse me," I said to our tour guide, "Can I touch that spider over there?"

"NO," warned the tour guide, "it can kill you."

After hearing that, I stayed with the group of people following the guide. There were many cool things in the mangroves.

When we got back to the beach, I went snorkelling a bit farther out so I could catch some big boat wakes! I managed to catch a few big ones, one from a panga, and one from a kayuko, a local style boat carved out of one tree. The other was from a party boat, just starting its afternoon party.

I swam back to the beach, and packed up all my stuff. Our bus zoomed around the corner from Starfish Beach; it felt like it was out of control. I peered at the passing jungle, it looked beautiful! I was glad I was staying here!

Tomorrow I was going to find a property, an island I wanted. I was going to go looking with a real estate agent, his name was Mark.

When I got back to the hotel I sat down for a while, then went to dinner at Tropical Bird. I had a great sleep that night!

The next morning I met Mark at the Rip Tide, a

floating restaurant. After lots of chatting, we started on our journey to find a nice island.

First, we went to look at an island that was by Isla Bastimentos, very close to a restaurant called Roots. I liked the island but was not in love with it. After that, we went to look at an island about 25 minutes from town. It was at the north entrance of a bay called Dolphin Bay.

I loved this island; there were lots of plants and it was only 2 acres.

I told Mark I wanted this island and he asked, "Are you sure you do not want to see any other places?"

"No!" I replied. "I want this one, it's perfect!" It was a very reasonable price.

Chapter 2

Time to Start Building

I was so happy! I had finally bought a property in a tropical place. I wanted to start building a house immediately, but there were some challenges I had to deal with first.
1). Get a boat.
2). Get building materials.
3). I had to go to David.
4). I needed to hire some workers to clear the island.
5). I needed to make some friends!

I tried to get back in touch with Mark and successfully did. I asked him if he knew of anyone selling a boat for a decent price, or if he knew where I could get a cheap new boat. He said he didn't have one in mind, but thought I could get a big kayuko with a 50 horse power engine for around $6000.

I said I would do that and we went to a little local house with a couple kayukos tied up out front, on Isla Caranero. I got a sturdy, well painted kayuko with an engine for $6100. I had done the first step of owning a tropical island, getting a local styled boat. This meant I could actually get to the island.

After that, Mark and I went out for coffee at the Rip Tide. After we were done our coffee, we said farewell and I thanked Mark very much!

That night I stayed at Hotel Los Brisas, owned by a gringo named Andy.

Chapter 3

Meeting Friends

I woke up the next morning. I had had a good sleep! Today I was going to try and get another step done from my tropical island list, if possible. I was not sure where to start, so I thought about trying to meet some gringo friends. I thought I should camp out at the Rip Tide for a bit, waiting for some people to show up. This way, I could have some friends.

A coffee later, many boats started coming and gringos started to fill the Rip Tide. I started talking to a guy, his name was Captain Ron. I told him I had just bought the property at the north entrance of Dolphin Bay. Captain Ron introduced me to some other people too. Their names were Bruce, Cynde, Kent, Marci, Terry, and some other people, but I couldn't remember all their names. I thanked Captain Ron kindly and went to wander around town for a bit.

I did not find anything interesting around town. All I did was get some cereal from the one gourmet store in Bocas. Then I went to the town beach. I hung there for a bit, then bought a Honka Honka from a guy biking around with a cart!

A Honka Honka is shaved ice, with fruity syrup and a couple drops of condensed milk. I call them Honka Honkas but you probably don't. The reason I call them Honka Honkas is because all the carts the vendors ride around on have horns that make a Honking noise.

I was very hot and decided to go back to my hotel and go into my air conditioned room. I stayed there for a bit, not knowing what to do. I read my book for a while and eventually I fell asleep. That was my day over.

Chapter 4

Who Do I Ask?

I woke up to find another morning of icky, brown cockroaches crawling all over the floor. I could barely put my foot down without stepping on one. I've hated roaches ever since I saw my first one!

I got dressed and went up to the Rip Tide to get some breakfast. I had a yummy combo of hash browns, eggs and toast. After that I thought about hiring some locals to trim all the fern-like things on the island.

"Who could I ask?" I said to Captain Ron.

"I know who you can ask," Cynde chimed in. "There is a local guy. His name is Fernando. He will do your work well. Just do not pay him until he is finished the work. I will help you find him!"

"Thank you!" I said to Cynde. After that Cynde and I went off into town to find Fernando.

"There he is." yelled Cynde. We walked up to him and Fernando had a chat with Cynde in Spanish.

"Okay, he is ready to work tomorrow. He will work for one week. If you need him to work for more than a week just get in touch with me!"

I thanked Cynde very much.

"I would not have been able to do it alone." I told her.

Chapter 5

A Nice Day at the Island

The next day I went in my boat to the island. Fernando was already there cutting ferns.
I said, "¿Como estas?" in my bad Spanish. He made a silent laugh and corrected all of my pronunciations!
I did not know what to do, but then I remembered I had borrowed some snorkelling gear from Mark. So I went snorkelling. It was much more exciting than Starfish Beach, because there were more than just starfish. It was the best snorkelling I had done in weeks!
My favourite thing that I saw was a wavy looking creature. I didn't know what it was called, but I think it was some kind of sea worm. When I touched it, it sucked in and disappeared! When I touched them it felt like wet feathers. I also saw many cool fish with lots of bright colours on them.
I went back on land to see how work was going. It was not going well. Fernando was sitting at a table eating one of *my* island coconuts.
"¿Qué está haciendo?" I asked.
"Mi machete oxidado es que necesito una nueva."
"Mañana, cuando estás en la ciudad por una nueva." I said.
"Me compre un machete nuevo." Fernando replied.
I walked off. I was not going to buy Fernando a machete. I was definitely not giving him money to buy one. He would probably use it for beer and have a hangover tomorrow and not show up at work. I was not taking that risk.
I was about to go back to town when some nice folks showed up. Steve and Jeanne handed me a batch of fabulous cookies, to welcome me to Bocas. I thanked them very much. We chatted for a while.

When I headed back to town, I went to hotel Los Brisas and went to sleep. I was still not sure if I should buy a machete for Fernando.

Chapter 6

Exploring the Area

The next morning I woke up and went to a Chino store to get some stuff for lunch at the island. I got yogurt, a small mango and cereal. I put it in the cooler I had bought a couple days ago.

I set off in my boat to my island. It was a bit choppy but my kayuko handled it fine! It cut through the waves very well. I had bought Fernando a machete, though I did not know if it was a good choice.

When I got to the island Fernando was eating his breakfast. I gave him the machete and he smiled at me kindly. I thought I should explore the area a bit, so I went to look at Dolphin Bay.

Dolphin Bay was a little protected area, with lots of houses at the water's edge. I saw some a sail boat mast and thought, "That must be a gringo house". No locals owned sail boats.

Hoping to meet some neighbours, I went in and out of all the small mangrove cuts trying to get to the house. When I had found my way through all the confusing mangrove cuts, I was finally at the neighbour's house. I parked my boat at their dock and went and knocked on their door.

A friendly couple named Pam and Bruce opened the door. They were house-sitting for a couple named Bill and Janis, who were in the States at the moment.

There was one sail boat parked outside the house. On it there was a couple named Evan and Monique. Their boat was named *Margarita*.

Bruce and Pam invited me to dinner even though we had just met! I said hi to Evan and Monique and went back to the island.

Fernando had done a good job, but if he kept going at the same rate he would not get it done for the end of the week.

"You need to go faster," I told him.

"Okay," he replied.

"Start now," I told him.

So he did. The jungle on the island was very thick, so thick you could not walk around it without walking into spider webs and other bug nests!

Docks - the island had one dock. It was made out of wood that was rotting and had no roof on it. My future plan was to eventually build a rock dock, but first I was going to hire some people to put a roof on the wood dock and some better wood.

I was going to get Cynde to help me hire some workers to build the dock. The next day I went to Cynde's house and asked if she could help me find some workers to build a roof on the wood dock. She said she would!

The next morning Cynde and I went to a couple local houses, asking if any of the local people wanted a job. Some already had jobs, but some said "Yes." Cynde said I would pay them $10 a day. I thought that was too little, but Cynde said everyone paid that or less. So I went with it!

I got building materials from a little hardware store called Chow Kai. I got lots of wood and red tin for the dock's roof. I also got things like nails, screws, glue, three machetes and all that building stuff.

The next day I loaded all the building materials in my big kayuko and set off to the island.

Half an hour later, when I got to the island, there were a whole bunch of workers waiting for me. They unloaded all the stuff that I had bought the day before, with ease. They started working and work went fast. Well, fast for here.

The dock was done in a week. It looked stable, but I did figure out why the pay is only ten dollars a day. The nails were sticking out and not one of the boards was even close to being straight.

I had given my workers their pay every day. One or two times a worker would ask me for some extra money, but I said "No." I explained that I had no extra money. I had been told to be careful about lending money in Bocas.

I was proud of myself. I knew I had not done much, but it sure felt like it!

Chapter 7

One Year Later

I had built my house successfully and was living in it! Many frustrating things happened in that time, between the dock creation and getting the house done. I will tell you one thing that happened to me on the way. It's kind of funny.
One day I was going to a restaurant called Rana Azul. It is a restaurant in the jungle, with great wood fired oven pizza and other amazing foods. I go there every Sunday.
I had a great journey there and was planning to have a great journey back! I was still chatting, when I realized the only people still hanging out were the people that lived five minutes away. I ran to the bartender (Junior) and asked him what time it was. He calmly said 6:00pm.
"Yikes, I usually go home at 5:00pm." I said in my head. I quickly paid the bill and ran down the dock! I jumped in my little boat and tried to start it, but it took about 11 pulls to get it running well.
I love bugs and animals and that didn't help. There was a gecko in the boat. I had to take the time to let it go!
I put the boat on full throttle. As soon as I got to the gap between the Dark Lands and Dolphin Bay, it all went black. The mangroves looked like they had all been suddenly put together. I couldn't find the cuts to get through. I stopped the boat. I had totally lost my bearings!
I headed up to what I thought was the top of Dolphin Bay. I reached it sooner than I thought I would reach it, and stopped suddenly. I panicked, not knowing what to do. I took some deep breaths and listened to the waves gently rocking the boat back and forth. I looked around the area to see if there were any lights in sight.
I saw one.
"Yeah", I thought, as I steered my boat slowly toward

the light. Before I got there I noticed it was a boat.

On board Second Star, there were two friendly passengers. Their names were Johne and Aeon. I went aboard their boat and asked them a big favour.

"Can I stay a night on your boat? I got lost coming back from the Dark Lands and can't find my way back to my island."

They said, "Of course".

I slept on their guest bed.

In the morning I asked for some directions and they told me where I had to go. I had to get home quickly to control the Bocas Net. I said I would call them on the radio sometime and they could come have dinner on the island one day. They said that would be great and waved me off.

Chapter 8

Bocas Net and Other Things

I drove home quickly and got ready to control the Bocas Net.

The Bocas Emergency Network is available seven days a week. If you have an emergency you can say that on the radio and there will be lots of nice people wanting to help you! Each morning the net is controlled from 7:45-8:15. At that time, you can announce general announcements, events, anything you want to sell or give away, and boat problems and tips.

I was the Monday net controller. There are other nets in other places, but this net was very unique because it also included people on land. Most nets are only for people on sail boats and other types of vessels.

Every person on land had a Ben number. I was Ben 63. I enjoyed being the net controller.

On my days as net controller, I would go through all the usual categories. ...local weather report done by Captain Ron, general check ins, new boats, returning boats, people that are leaving by planes, treasures (anything you want to give away sell or purchase), open forum (where you can say whatever you want). Every morning Jeffery would ask two trivia questions.

After the net, I had my breakfast. I was going to town. I packed my laundry, beer crate and propane bottle into the panga which I had bought a few days ago. I was off.

I parked my boat at Chow Kai, one of the three main hardware stores in Bocas. I did all my shopping and filled up propane. I was not planning to stay in town for long.

I went to get some gas and saw a really cute puppy. I wanted to take it home, but I knew couldn't! I filled all my tanks up and went home.

When I got into my bay I saw a local boy fishing about 2 meters from the dock. I made a point to notice him and started a conversation.

"Hola!"

The conversation did not get far. He hurried out of the bay as soon as he noticed me. Three months ago, my kayuko had gotten stolen from my dock, so I was more cautious now. I had found it parked outside a store in Loma Partida and had gotten it back, but I didn't want to lose it again.

I unloaded all my stuff from the boat and started making trips up to the house.

Once I was done bringing groceries up to the house, I cleaned out my little inflatable pool. I stayed in there for a while, not wanting to get out because the chitres would get me. Chitres are very little fly-like bugs, whose bites can get somewhat itchy. I stayed in the pool. I swam around but did not get far, of course.

Chapter 9

A Busy Social Calendar!

The next day, I had some breakfast at the island, then went to a friend Terry's place. He had offered to give me some sod.
 He gave me lots of sod! When I had loaded six bags of sod into my boat I went back to the island.
 I laid all the sod down around the house. It looked a lot better than just soggy mud.
 I was hot and sweaty, so I decided to go snorkelling. I saw a toad fish and lots of the usual fish. They were still very pretty, even though I had seen them many times! My favourite was a yellow fish that was tall and not very long. It had a dot in the middle of its body; it looked like an eye!
 I went back in and changed. I looked at my calendar.
 "OH!" I shouted.
 Today I was supposed to go to my friend Wayne's house. He lived down in Loma Partida, a very nice area about one hour away from my island.
 I jumped in my panga. With some brownies in hand, I zoomed to his house.
 When I got there, he gave me a tour of the farm. I could just picture dinosaurs roaming around it! He had adult goats, one baby goat, chickens, and rabbits. Guess what, he even had toucans! He had a male and a female. Whenever I picked one up, it would grab onto my bright red floatation device with its big multi-coloured beak. They were both beautiful; I wanted to keep one.
 I stayed there for a while and a nice couple named Peter and Jane showed up. We chatted and ate passion fruit brownies! When the clock turned to 5:00pm, I made my way back to my island.
 Campesino, my guard dog, was waiting for me on the

dock. He started yapping joyfully as I jumped on to the dock and tied my boat up.

I went back to my house to find two freshly laid island eggs, one tan and one white. They were left by my two laying hens, Gina and Brownie.

Gina is a very pretty chicken, she is all different colours. Brownie has feathers that look like a peacock but she is brown. Big Red, my rooster, and my two white meat hens, were scratching the ground looking for bugs.

When I got to the house I crashed on my couch.

Chapter 10

Tiles

The one thing I did not have in my house was tiles. However, having heard many frustrating stories of bad customer service in David, I personally did not want to go. David was the only place with big tile stores.

I was planning to go to David, in a couple days, for tiles. I planned to go for two days, thinking I would not need that much time just to get a couple packs of tiles. I planned to stay one night in Boquete, a nice mountain town with lots of coffee plantations and beautiful views.

The first day, after two long bus rides from Bocas, I stayed at a nice hotel called Pension Marilas. The owners were very nice. They had nice clean rooms looking out onto the mountains and coffee plantations. It was one of the most beautiful hotels I had been to here in Panama.

I spent my day in Boquete walking around and taking photos of every nice view I could find. I went to a nice restaurant by the mountains and had a fabulous meal.

The next morning I got on the bus to go to David. The bus ride wasn't very long, but you had to deal with the occasional chicken squawk.

When the bus finally got to David, I went to the hotel I had in mind. Hotel Chiriqui looked nice from the pictures on the internet. It was a nice hotel, maybe not the best view, but probably the best room you could get in David!

I stayed in my hotel for about twenty minutes, looking up other places to buy tiles apart from Do It Centre and Novey. I found a couple others. I slowly made my way out of my hotel room, to a taxi.

I went to the Do It Centre first. I found a great combination of tiles there, borders and all. I started to order my tiles.

When I got to the border tiles they said "We don't have those." I asked why they were still on the shelf even though they were out of stock. The guy just shrugged. I decided to go to Novey.

When I got to Novey, I went to the tile section. They had better quality tiles, not the best, but the prices were very, very high! I looked at all the tiles there. The only thing I saw that I could afford was a nice border, with lots of colourful fish and sea grass! I was not sure if I should get it or not, taking the risk of not finding other tiles to match. I decided to order them anyway, they were perfect.

I went back to the Do It Centre, hoping to find a set of tiles that would match the border tiles I had just bought. I found some pretty good combinations. I ordered some sandy feeling floor tiles for the bathroom. They were a dark grey. For the walls, I ordered a nice light blue tile.

It was about 7:00pm when I had finished all that tile shopping. Tomorrow I had to do more. I dreaded tomorrow.

The next morning I got some fruit for breakfast, then went to a tile store called El-mec. The only tiles I still had to get were kitchen counter tiles and living room floor tiles. I knew El-mec was going to be quite expensive, but I found tiles for the living room floor that were not too expensive. However, I did not find tiles for the kitchen counters.

I decided to go back to Do It Centre for the rest of the tiles I needed. I got there and ordered some nice tiles with different shades of brown in them. They were not too sandy, but still quite grippy.

I looked at my phone. It was 10:00am. I had to catch a bus at 11:30am. I also had to meet Toby's sister to give her my receipts. Toby brings things\orders from David to Bocas by truck. Her sister was going to pick up my receipts. Toby's sister was surprisingly late. When I had called Toby she said her sister would meet me in a couple minutes. Those minutes turned into over one hour.

When Toby's sister finally came it was 11:10. I now had about twenty to tweny-five minutes to get on the bus back to Bocas. I rushed back to the hotel in which I was staying, grabbed all my stuff, and checked out as fast as I could.

The bus station was three or four blocks away and David is very busy on a sunny day. I dodged many cars, loads of people carrying big boxes and lots of other things! I got to the bus station without a minute to spare. I bought a bottle of water, then quickly jumped on the bus!

Four hours later, the bus stopped in Alimirante. I had to catch a water taxi from there to Bocas. I got to go on a little water taxi. It was very calm and we zoomed along the water. We got to Bocas in about twenty minutes.

My boat was parked at Hotel Las Brisas, where someone was watching it for me. I got a little bit of shopping, then headed back to the island. Campesino was waiting on the dock for me. He yapped joyfully once he saw that it was me!

By the time I had gotten into the house, it was 5:00pm. I cooked rice and beans with hot sauce. I hung out for a while reading, then went to bed.

Chapter 11

A Breakfast with Johne and Aeon

"Hey!" I yelled, from my panga. I was just on my way to town and happened to see Second Star coming out of the anchorage.

"Hey!" Aeon yelled back.

"Where are you guys going?" I asked.

"We are going to stay four nights in Dolphin Bay again, we really like it."

"Would you guys like to come for dinner at the island in a couple days?"

"We'd love to." yelled Aeon.

I said I would call them on the radio when I got back home.

I went to town and got groceries for two and a half weeks. When I was done shopping, I started on my journey back home. It was quite rough, but could have been much worse.

Twenty-five minutes later, I got to my island. I quickly unloaded my groceries in fear it might start raining soon. When I got up to the house, I unpacked all the groceries. I thought I would be able to go for three weeks if I wanted.

What am I going to do tomorrow I wondered? There were many things I could do. I hoped it would be a nice calm day, so I could go somewhere in the boat.

The next morning, I jumped out of bed. I was going to go snorkelling at a new spot that I had found on Google Earth! On the map it looked like there was a lagoon right by it. I was not sure if there was a cut into it or not.

I set out to find the lagoon very early in the morning. I got to the place I was looking for. There were no cuts. I had brought my water shoes in case there would be mangroves to climb through. I tied my boat to a thick mangrove branch and started my climb! When I got half way I could tell that there was closed in water.

After slowly picking my way through the mangroves I got to the lagoon.

"There must be some big fish in here", I thought.

I jumped in for a swim. I got out very fast once I realized it was a natural jellyfish hatchery. There was every type of jellyfish I could think of, and millions of them! I wouldn't go swimming in that lagoon anymore.

I did go snorkelling just outside it. There were some fantastic corals and a couple big Barracudas. I got back in my boat and zoomed toward my house. It was very rough on the way back, but my little boat handled it quite well!

On the way back something did happen. When I was about one kilometre from my house, I ran out of fuel.

"How is that?" I wondered. The engine was doing fine when I left, but it was now using twice the fuel it should have been. Something must have happened to it on the way to the lagoon.

Well, my neighbour's house was close. I could stop and get my fuel can that they had borrowed. I got my flippers on and jumped off the boat. I held onto the back of the boat and pushed it. It took about forty minutes to get to Kent and Marci's house.

When I finally got there, they said they had used all the fuel and hadn't been able to get to town to replace it. So I used their radio to call Bruce (Ben 42). I asked him if he had some spare fuel that I could buy from him.

He said, "Yes" and brought it over. I said I would give Bruce a full tank next time I went to get some gas. I said bye to Kent, Marci and Bruce and went home.

The next day, I climbed into my big boat. It was time to go to Rana Azul! I stopped to get gas on the way there, in Dolphin Bay.

I idled my way up to the dock at Rana Azul. There were already five boats there. I've never been the first one to

Rana Azul! I jumped off the boat to be greeted by many nice friends. I chatted for a while, drinking my favourite Rana Azul drink, Ginger ale.

When it came to 1:04pm I ordered an order of fish and chips. The fish and chips were fantastic like always. I left just in time to get back home when the sun went down.

I set my alarm for 7:00 am, my usual time for Monday mornings. I woke up at 7:00am the next morning and scuttled out of my bed. I slowly made my morning tea, I also made my breakfast.

I finished my breakfast just in time to give the morning net call!

"Good morning Bocas and welcome to the Bocas net! The net will start in 15 minutes right here on channel 68. So make your morning drink, whatever it is, and get ready to participate on the net."

The net went slow. There was talk about garbage issues and robberies that had happened over night. As usual, a couple dinghies were stolen, and some other things, like backpacks. When I got to the shut-down, my fingers were sore from holding the radio button too much. I had finally finished the net!

After I had read a bit of my book, I called Second Star on the radio. They said they would come over tomorrow for breakfast instead of dinner. I said that would be fine. I told them to come over around 8:00am.

The rest of the day I planted gardens and raked the island. I also put some homemade bagels in the refrigerator to sit overnight, so they would be ready to bake for breakfast.

The next morning Johne and Aeon arrived on time for breakfast. The bagels were just ready to eat! We sat and chatted, eating yummy bagels and a large array of tropical fruits.

9:00am came and they said they should head back to their boat. They had to finish some projects they had started earlier that morning. I waved them away at my dock very fast so I did not get eaten alive by chitres. I packed the remaining fruit in a big zip lock bag and put it in the freezer, for the next time I made a smoothie!

Chapter 12

A Nice Horse Adventure

A week later, I went to visit some friends, Dave and Molly. Dave guided horse riding tours through the jungle. I was going to go on the tour.

The tour went like this. First we would ride through the jungle, then we would stop at a village for lunch and hang out for a while, then we would go back to his house. I would get to ride on a beautiful Pasofino, whose name was Tongo. He was a nice horse.

We got on our horses and started riding in the jungle. After about fifteen minutes we climbed up a ridge. There was a beautiful view at the top of the ridge. Dave showed me where my house was. I took some photos and we kept on going.

Thirty minutes later, we rode out onto the village's baseball field. We tied the horses on posts and went to see the village. We got a nice lunch of chicken, rice, plantains and lentils. When we had finished our lunch, we walked around the village for a while.

Soon we were heading back to the horses. We jumped on our horses and headed back to Dave's house. The trail was fun, with lots of up and downs and obstacles to get over!

When we got back to Dave's house, we unsaddled the horses and chatted for a while. After that I went into town to go grocery shopping. That did not take very long, and I was soon driving back to the island.

Campesino was waiting for me on the dock, as I slowly pulled up. I grabbed the wheelbarrow from the pathway. I always left it there, but not too close to the dock, so you could not see it from the water.

I managed to fit two fuel cans and all my groceries in the wheelbarrow. It was about 5:00pm and the chitres were horrendous. I was glad I could fit all the groceries in the wheelbarrow at once.

I unpacked all my groceries and had my favourite dinner, a big bowl of Breakfast Muesli Cereal. I finished my cereal fast and watched two episodes of my favourite TV series, on my computer. That night I fell asleep on the couch.

The next morning when I woke up, my legs were surprisingly not sore at all from riding! I did not know what I was going to do today. I started working on the island and planting some plants in the garden. I planted basil, hot peppers, onions, tomatoes and radishes.

In the afternoon it started to rain. I was glad, because my tank was not very full. The way I get fresh water is to collect it from my roof, with a pipe system. It had not rained in two and a half weeks, and I wanted to get some water for my gardens!

I hung inside for a while reading and writing, on my computer. It rained from 3:00pm all the way until midnight! My tank was full and it was still raining! I had to go bail my little boat about three times, in the pouring rain. When the rain finally finished I went to bed!

I woke up the next morning and went downstairs to feed the chickens. The island was soaked. It looked really soaked because it was high tide. I did not have to give the chickens any water today.

I had breakfast and listened to the Bocas Net. When the net was over, I went snorkelling. I saw a beautiful fish. It was blue and had shiny dots and yellow fins and tail. I graded it as the number one tropical fish. When I got back to the dock I jumped in my small kayuko and went for a little paddle to the rock dock.

I saw a round stingray that was white with brown spots. I got pretty close to it in my kayuko. I also saw an octopus, but it hid under a rock before I could get a really good look at it.

I stayed out on the water until 10:00am because it was flat calm and the views were beautiful I went on a little route I had made up: I would paddle to the rock dock, then out to a stick where it was very deep, a bit further toward another dock, and finally back into the wood dock with all the motor boats.

The sun was hot, but there were some nice shady spots on the island to hang out by. I did the same as yesterday and also did some raking. My favourite part of working on the island was trimming the trees. I do the not-so-fun work first, which includes raking and chopping ferns, then I move onto the fun things.

I had pasta with veggies and sauce that night. Then I went to bed.

Chapter 13

Kathy's Party

Kathy lives in Loma Partida, a very nice area with lots of fun gringos and locals living there. Kathy lives in a nice, bright yellow house on the water. I was going there today for a party.

I packed brownies and all my swimming gear. When I got to Kathy's house I jumped in, eager for a nice cool swim, after the hot boat ride. Lots of people jumped in, others got pushed in. There were lots of yummy finger foods. I had some great conversations with Peter and Jane and Chocolate Dave. Chocolate Dave told me a great story of an Ocelot he once had.

After hanging out for a while by the house, I went to look around Kathy's property. It was a steep hill with lots of cool plants and lots of Fire Ants! I came back with some questions.

I only mentioned one, which was, "What's the big round, green thing on the big, green bush?"

Kathy answered my question and said it was called calabaso. It could be used for making bowls and other things such as flower pots, bird feeders, or boat bailers. She asked if I would like to take one home and make a bowl.

Always excited for a new project I said, "Yes".

Kathy told me I had to take a spoon and scrape all the white flesh out, then wash it and let it dry. Ta-dah, you have a calabaso bowl! I said thank you and put the big calabaso in my boat.

The rest of the afternoon was the same, pushing people in and going for a swim. When I thought I should probably leave, I looked at the clock and it was 5:20pm. I quickly gathered my stuff and drove off. I got back just as it was getting dark.

When I got back I read for a while, and had a bowl of my favourite cereal. After reading about twenty long chapters, I went to bed.

Epilogue

Well, I had done what I aimed to do and was quite happy. There are lots of great reasons about living here. Here I will give you some little examples.
    1). Lots of nice friendly people to hang out with
    2). The nice hot climate
    3). Lot of places to have a good adventure
    4).The privilege to say that you own a tropical property in the Caribbean

I had made very good friends, and never wanted to even think about leaving.

About The Author

My name is Maible Matrishon.

I am 9 years old. I live in Whitehorse, Yukon, Canada.

For the past two years my mom, my brother and I have been coming down to stay in Bocas Del Toro, Panama during the winter months.

My stepdad owns an island, where we spend time when we are here. Because we have so many funny and adventurous things that happen to us down here, I thought that it would be a great place about which to write a story.

Additional material and photographs illustrating "Island Experiences" available at:-

MaibleMatrishon.com

www.ingramcontent.com/pod-product-compliance
Lightning Source LLC
Chambersburg PA
CBHW031439040426
42444CB00006B/884